first book of
tractors
and trucks

Isabel Thomas

For Harry, Joey and Oscar

Published 2013 by
A&C Black
An imprint of Bloomsbury Publishing Plc
50 Bedford Square, London, WC1B 3DP

www.bloomsbury.com

ISBN 978-1-4081-9292-4

A CIP catalogue for this book is available from the British Library.

Printed in China by C&C.

10 9 8 7 6 5 4 3 2 1

Contents

Truck and tractor safety
Trucks and tractors are powerful machines. They can be very
dangerous. Always have an adult with you when you look at
trucks and tractors. Do not stand close to trucks and tractors.
Do not walk behind a truck or tractor. Make sure the driver
can see you. Never touch a truck or tractor.

Tractors and trucks

Every tractor and truck has a job to do.
Look out for tractors pulling huge farm
machines. Listen out for the rumble of a
mixer truck, or a fire engine's siren.

You can spot trucks and tractors on the
road. You can see them hard at work on
building sites and farms. This book will help
you to name the trucks and tractors you
see. It tells you how they work. It shows
you what special features to look out for.

At the back of this book is a Spotter's Guide
to help you remember the tractors and
trucks you find. Tick them off as you spot
them. You can also find out the meaning of
some useful words here.

Turn the page to find out all about tractors
and trucks!

Two-wheel-drive tractor

A tractor is one of the most useful machines on a farm. It can pull and lift heavy loads. Look out for simple tractors like this on small farms.

Large back wheels

Exhaust pipe

The engine powers the back wheels.

Cab

The small front wheels turn to steer the tractor.

Small front wheels help the tractor steer around tight corners

Four-wheel-drive tractor

Big farms need heavy, powerful tractors. The engine powers all four wheels. This helps the tractor to push or pull very big loads.

Tractors make it easier to do jobs like ploughing, planting and harvesting crops.

Cab

Exhaust

Headlight

Mudguard

Four large wheels

Large wheels stop the tractor slipping or getting stuck in mud.

Fire engine

Fire engines work hard. They carry
firefighters quickly to emergencies.
They pump water through hoses to
put out fires. They also carry rescue
gear, such as tools,
ropes and ladders.

Flashing
lights

Nozzle

Water
gun

Pumper engines carry water in
a huge tank. They can suck up
extra water from fire hydrants.

Cab

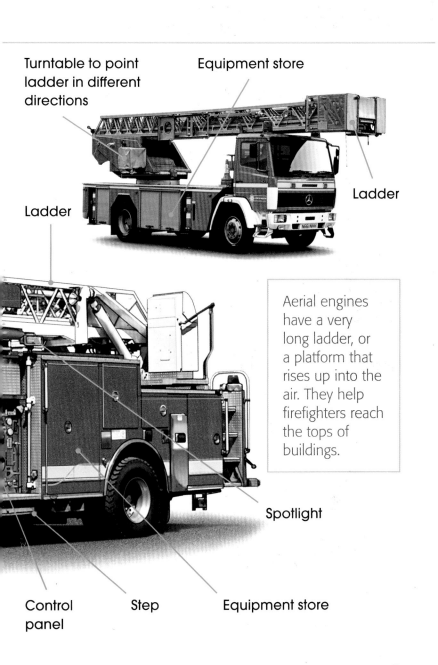

Turntable to point ladder in different directions

Equipment store

Ladder

Ladder

Aerial engines have a very long ladder, or a platform that rises up into the air. They help firefighters reach the tops of buildings.

Spotlight

Control panel

Step

Equipment store

Articulated lorry

This huge truck has two parts. The driver's cab and engine are in the tractor at the front. Goods are carried in the trailer at the back.

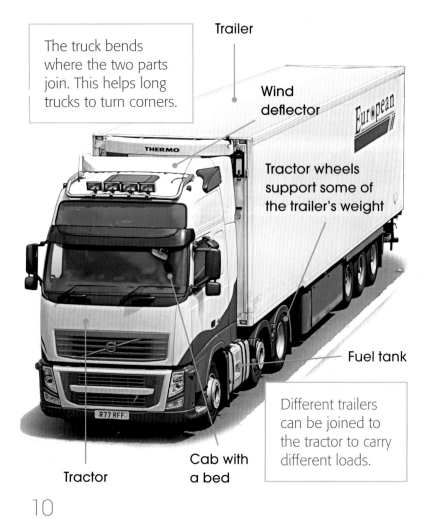

Trailer

The truck bends where the two parts join. This helps long trucks to turn corners.

Wind deflector

THERMO

European

Tractor wheels support some of the trailer's weight

Fuel tank

Different trailers can be joined to the tractor to carry different loads.

Cab with a bed

Tractor

R77 RFF

Telehandler

A bale of straw can weigh as much as a small car. Telehandlers can move and stack these huge bales.

The arm slides out like a telescope. It can reach the top of a large stack.

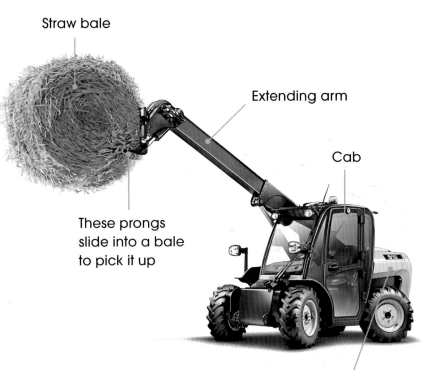

Straw bale

Extending arm

Cab

These prongs slide into a bale to pick it up

Counterweight

Mixer truck

This truck delivers concrete. Cement, sand, gravel, and water are tipped into the drum. The drum turns as the truck drives along. This mixes the concrete.

When the truck gets to the building site, the concrete is ready to pour.

Chute for pouring concrete

Mixing drum

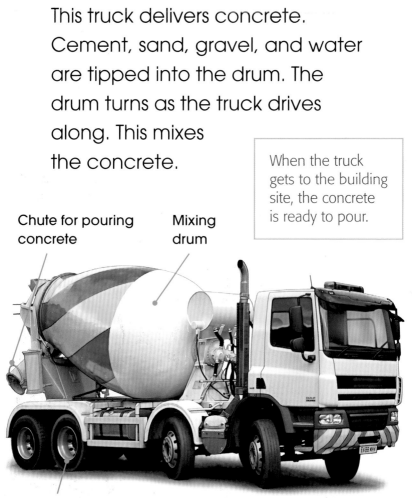

Extra wheels to spread the weight of the truck

The drum spins in both directions. One way mixes concrete. The other moves concrete out of the drum.

Tanker

These trucks have huge tanks. Some carry liquids, such as fuel and milk. Some transport powders, such as flour. Others carry gases.

This fuel tanker is divided up inside. It can carry different fuels at the same time.

Manholes to get inside the tanks

Hazard label warns that the load is dangerous

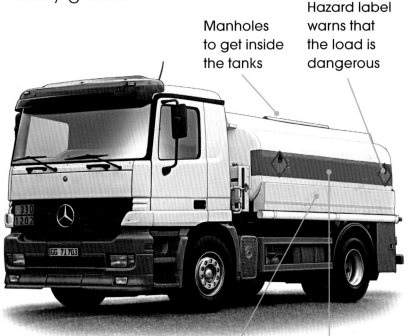

Pipes stored at the side of the tank for delivering fuel

Metal tank

Articulated tractor

An articulated tractor bends in the middle. This helps it turn tight corners quickly. It can work in small spaces. It saves the farmer time.

Engine powers all four wheels

Wheels are all the same size

Tractor bends at this joint

This tractor can steer between rows of plants in orchards and greenhouses.

Armoured truck

Trucks like this carry money. They deliver to banks, shops, and cash machines. Special features keep the driver, guard and cargo safe.

The police and armed forces also use armoured trucks.

CCTV records what happens inside the truck

Bulletproof glass

Steel walls, floor, roof and doors

Small, sealed windows

Sloping windscreen

Wheels keep running even when the tyres are flat

Large, tough bumper

Radiator guard

Utility tractor

Utility tractors do lots of different jobs. The farmer attaches different machines to the front and back. He controls everything from the cab.

This tractor has a loader. It scoops, lifts, and moves heavy loads.

Roll bar

Mudguard

Large back wheel

Blade for levelling ground

Deep treads for driving over rough or muddy ground

Step for climbing into cab

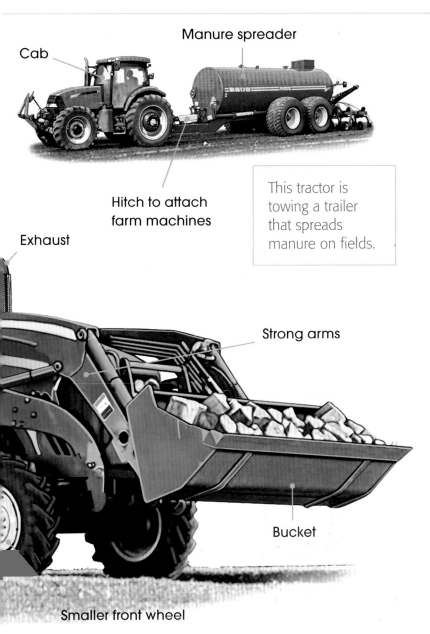

Manure spreader

Cab

Hitch to attach
farm machines

This tractor is
towing a trailer
that spreads
manure on fields.

Exhaust

Strong arms

Bucket

Smaller front wheel

Dumper

You can see dumpers on building sites. They can carry huge loads of earth and rubble. To empty the truck, pistons lift one end of the truck bed. The load slides out quickly.

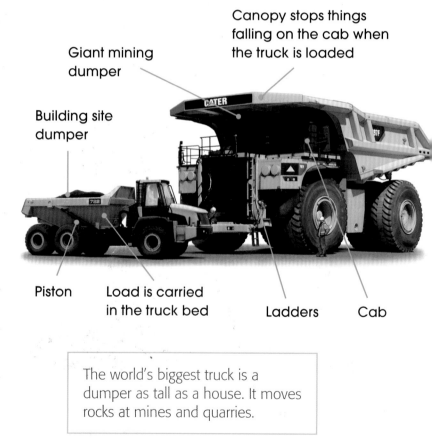

Canopy stops things falling on the cab when the truck is loaded

Giant mining dumper

Building site dumper

Piston

Load is carried in the truck bed

Ladders

Cab

The world's biggest truck is a dumper as tall as a house. It moves rocks at mines and quarries.

Walking tractor

Tractors with two wheels can be used to farm small areas of land. The tractor pushes or pulls small farm machines. The farmer steers by walking behind.

Look out for walking tractors being used to cut grass or clear snow.

They make it easier to do jobs such as ploughing, watering and weeding.

Handlebars

Controls on the handles

Fuel tank

Petrol or diesel engine

Two wheels

Small farm machine

19

Car transporter

Loading a car transporter is like doing a big jigsaw. Each car is driven on to a platform. The platforms are tilted to fit as many cars as possible on the truck.

Most transporters carry new cars from factories to car shops.

Ramps are lowered to get cars on and off

Driver's cab

Cars are held in place with chains or straps

Antique tractor

Very old tractors are called antique tractors. Some are still used on farms. You can also see them at special shows.

This old tractor has three wheels. This helps the farmer to drive between rows of crops without crushing the plants.

Petrol engine

Metal seat

One front wheel

Spacing of back wheels can be changed to fit different-sized rows

Ambulance

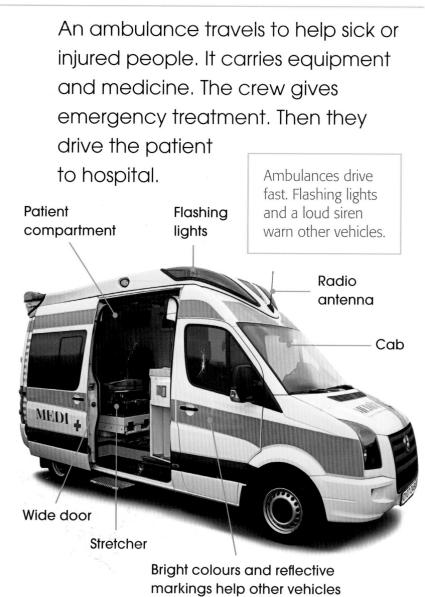

An ambulance travels to help sick or injured people. It carries equipment and medicine. The crew gives emergency treatment. Then they drive the patient to hospital.

Ambulances drive fast. Flashing lights and a loud siren warn other vehicles.

Patient compartment

Flashing lights

Radio antenna

Cab

MEDI +

Wide door

Stretcher

Bright colours and reflective markings help other vehicles to see the ambulance

Road sweeper

This truck works hard to keep roads and footpaths clean. Spinning brushes sweep litter, leaves and dirt into the truck's path. Everything is sucked up into a collection tank.

The trucks use a blast of water or air to loosen dirt.

Cab

Collection tank

Brush

Water tank

Crop tractor

Some tractors have a special shape. They are used to look after different types of crops.

The narrow tyres of this high crop tractor fit between rows of plants.

Tractor body is high above the ground so it does not squash tall vegetables

**Short cab can pass
under high branches**

This narrow tractor can drive through orchards without bumping into the trees.

Pick-up truck

This small truck has plenty of space for cargo. Pick-up trucks are tough. They can carry large loads and tow heavy trailers.

The tailgate can be flapped down or taken off. This makes it easy to load and unload the truck.

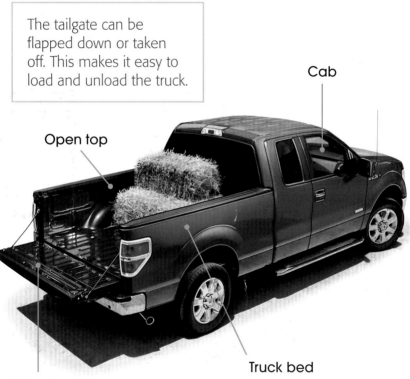

Cab

Open top

Truck bed

Tailgate

Monster truck

You won't spot a monster truck on the motorway! These huge vehicles are built for sport. They race and perform stunts.

Huge tyres let monster trucks jump, bounce and spin.

Body shaped like a pick-up truck

Body raised very high off ground

Fibreglass body

Scrap cars

Springs cushion the truck body from bumps

They can drive over anything in their path!

Huge tyres

Lightweight frame made of metal tubes

Winter service vehicle

Gritters, snow ploughs and snow blowers keep roads free of snow and ice. They are mounted on large trucks or tractors. Look out for them in freezing weather.

Hopper full of sand and salt

Snow ploughs push snow to one side of the road.

Snow plough

Spreader scatters grit across the whole road

Gritters spread a mixture of salt and sand. The salt helps to melt ice and snow. The sand helps tyres to grip the road.

Skiploader

Skips are huge bins. They can hold lots of heavy waste. Special trucks deliver empty skips, and collect them when they are full.

Skiploaders can lift and carry enormous loads.

Loading arm

Strong chains

Warning light

Skip

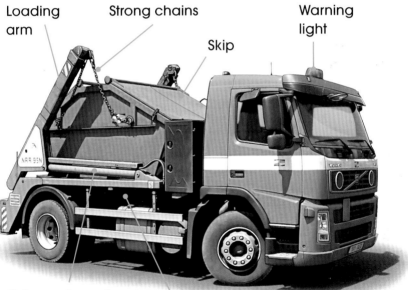

Pistons raise or lower the loading arms

Platform

The loading arms swing backwards to lift a skip from the truck onto the ground. They swing forwards to lift a skip onto the truck.

Crawler tractor

Tracks spread weight over a big area of ground. This stops the tractor from sinking into soft mud or snow. Crawler tractors are also good at climbing steep slopes.

Exhaust

Metal tracks

The driver steers by slowing the tracks on one side. The tracks on the other side keep moving.

Flatbed truck

Huge logs, heavy machines, and even houses can all be carried on flatbed trucks. These trucks have a large, flat platform. There is no roof or sides.

There may be a grabber arm to lift objects on and off. This is easy when there are no sides.

Platform

Cab

Load is tied down with straps or chains

Refuse collector

Refuse trucks collect rubbish. They crush and squeeze the rubbish so it takes up less space. More can be packed into the truck.

This truck is loaded from the back. Some are loaded from the front or side.

Steps help crew get on and off quickly

Rubbish is crushed inside the packer body

Then they take the
waste to be burned,
buried or recycled.

The crusher is
strong enough
to squash a
refrigerator!

This blade
scoops up
the rubbish
and pushes
it into the
packer body

Mechanism to lift
and empty bins
into the hopper

Rubbish is tipped into
the loading hopper

Giant tractor

Extra wheels give this tractor more pulling power. Tractors like this are used on the biggest farms. They pull huge farm machines across enormous fields.

Exhaust

Mirrors to help the driver see behind the tractor

Headlights

9620

Tyres taller than an adult

Huge engine

Deep treads to grip bumpy or muddy ground

The farmer uses buttons in the cab to control machines attached to the tractor.

Horsebox

Look out for horseboxes of different shapes and sizes. They transport horses to sport events. Large horseboxes have a living and sleeping area for people, as well as horses.

Thick walls stop the horses getting too hot or cold

Cabin with kitchen and bunk beds

Windows with safety bars

Compartments for storing gear

Door becomes a ramp for horses to walk up

This horsebox can carry six horses. The horses travel standing up.

Recovery truck

Sometimes vehicles break down or have accidents. Recovery trucks come to the rescue! They tow or carry damaged vehicles to be mended.

Cylinders raise and lower the boom

Towing device to raise the front wheels of a vehicle off the ground

Arm (boom)

This truck has an arm that can get longer. It can reach vehicles that have left the road.

Lawn tractor

Look out for mini tractors at work in gardens and parks. This one has sharp blades underneath. They spin around to cut grass.

Different machines can be attached to make garden jobs easier.

Speed control

Driver's seat

Steering wheel

Shallow treads so the wheels don't dig into grass

Spinning blades

Safety cover

Mobile crane

This truck is also a powerful lifting machine. It drives to a building site. Then it changes into an enormous crane.

Extending arm (telescopic boom)

Cables

Hook

Driver's cab

Legs called outriggers fold out from each side. They spread the weight of the crane, and stop it from toppling over.

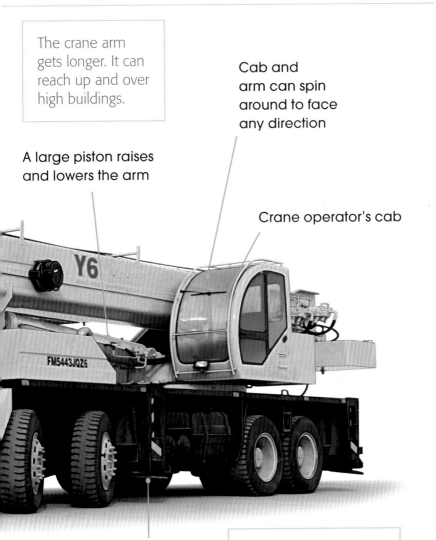

The crane arm gets longer. It can reach up and over high buildings.

Cab and arm can spin around to face any direction

A large piston raises and lowers the arm

Crane operator's cab

Y6

FM5443JQZ6

Outrigger

The crane arm (boom) is folded when the truck is driving.

Bus and coach

Buses and coaches can carry many passengers. This city bus carries people on short journeys. It has room for passengers to sit and stand.

Side mirror

Ticket reader

Route sign

Cab

Coaches carry people on longer journeys. They have comfortable seats with seat belts. There is no standing space.

Wide folding doors let passengers on and off quickly

Some have two decks to carry more passengers at a time.

Useful words

cab where the driver sits

chassis the metal frame that gives
a vehicle its shape

concrete a tough building material
that is mixed and poured, then sets
hard like rock

engine a machine inside a vehicle,
which burns fuel to make it go

exhaust a pipe that carries heat and
fumes away from an engine

mechanism parts that work together
inside a machine to do a certain job

ploughing breaking up hard ground
ready for planting

side mirror a mirror on the side of
a vehicle, to help the driver see
what is behind

tyre the soft rubber that covers wheels,
to help them grip the ground

Spotter's guide

How many of these tractors and trucks have you seen? Tick them when you spot them.

Two-wheel-drive tractor
page 6

Four-wheel-drive tractor
page 7

Fire engine
page 8

Articulated lorry
page 10

Telehandler
page 11

Mixer truck
page 12

Tanker
page 13

Articulated tractor
page 14

Armoured truck
page 15

Utility tractor
page 16

Dumper
page 18

Walking
tractor
page 19

Car transporter
page 20

Antique
tractor
page 21

Ambulance
page 22

Road
sweeper
page 23

Crop tractor
page 24

Pick-up truck
page 26

Monster truck
page 27

Winter service
vehicle
page 28

Skiploader
page 29

Crawler tractor
page 30

Flatbed truck
page 31

Refuse
collector
page 32

Giant tractor
page 34

Horsebox
page 35

Recovery truck
page 36

Lawn tractor
page 37

Mobile crane

Bus and coach

Find out more

If you would like to find out more about trucks and tractors, you could visit a farm museum or a transport museum. These websites are a good place to start.

The British Commercial Vehicle Museum
www.bcvmt.co.uk

Coventry Transport Museum
www.transport-museum.com

The Ulster Folk and Transport Museum
www.nmni.com/uftm